Would you rather...?'s

What's  Your Price...?

BECAUSE *Everyone* CAN BE *Bought!?*

Justin Heimberg & David Gomberg

Published by Falls Media
565 Park Avenue, Suite 11E
New York, NY 10021

First Printing, November 2007
10 9 8 7 6 5 4 3 2
© Copyright Justin Heimberg and David Gomberg, 2007
All Rights Reserved
Printed in Canada

Design by Tom Schirtz

ISBN-13 978-0-9788178-6-2

www.wouldyourather.com

To Ted DiBiase, the Million Dollar Man

HOW TO USE THIS BOOK

Sit around with a bunch of friends and read a question out loud. You can take turns answering questions or have everybody answer every question. These are the sorts of things we leave to you.

In either case, discuss the vices, virtues, and repercussions of each question and give your best honest answer amidst the laughing, gagging, and shame. For best effect, take time to visualize the questions, including context and reactions. Really think before answering and give a genuine answer. Truly consider them.

Usually, the first part of each question is "yes or no", but the follow-up questions take a little more thought. Answer each question individually before moving on to a follow-up question. We encourage you to let the questions be a springboard for conversation and self-examination. Though you may not always like what you discover...

TWO THINGS

A Special Note about Sex Questions

On occasion—many occasions actually—we ask if you'd have sex with someone or even something. If you are in a committed relationship, put that aside for the moment. Your significant other is not going to hold it against you if, for the purposes of this book, you say you'd give a happy ending to a koala bear for the chance to have sex with Angelina Jolie or Brad Pitt. So let it go and have fun.

Strike a Deal Questions

Every so often, you'll see a question that is tagged with "Strike a Deal!" This suggests that a deal or dare might be negotiated for real based on the questions given. Use the prices we give as a starting off point, and see what you can come up with. Pooling money is a good way to raise the necessary cash to get someone to do something entertaining like drink a bottle of ketchup or serenade a bank teller. Obviously, we are not responsible if you actually try to do any of the more dangerous or stupid things in this book; they are as the mantra goes: for entertainment purposes only.

THESE ARE THE CIRCUMSTANCES:

A powerful deity descends from on high, and for reasons beyond your understanding, informs you that you are about to face temptation. You will be presented with an opportunity that will test the boundaries of your conscience, measure your threshold for pain, or in some other fashion, determine the true nature of your character. Only you know the truth. Only you can decide if the money is worth it. Only you can answer...
What's Your Price?

ONE MORE THING

A Note About Prices

Throughout this book we ask you whether you would be willing to do something for a specified dollar amount. Would you, for example, iron your clothes while wearing them for $25,000? If the price we list is unacceptably low, don't just move on. Instead, take a minute to really think about the question, then name your own price...and there *will* be a price...there's *always* a price. Yes, 2nd degree burns from an iron might not be worth $25,000 to you, but for $250,000, perhaps you'd be able to deal with a little scorched and blistered skin. **EVERYONE CAN BE BOUGHT.**

All in the Family

Would you... wearing a mask, punch your grandmother as hard as you can in the stomach once for $10,000 if she never found out it was you? Would you do it for $100,000? $1,000,000?

What is the hardest you would punch her for $100,000? Demonstrate.

Would you... give two intense hickeys to your grandfather's neck for $2,000? Would it kill him?

Would you... make out with your sibling for two minutes for $5,000? One minute? 30 seconds? What would be your lowest dollar-per-second rate?

Would you... never communicate with your mother again for $1,000,000? What if you could communicate with her but only in free-style rap?

WHAT'S YOUR PRICE...?

The Price of Sex:
The "Add up to 100" Rule

(women) **Would you...** have sex with a 70 year old Marlon Brando to have sex with a 30 year old Marlon Brando? What two ages that add up to 100 would you choose?

(men) **Would you...** have sex with a future 75 year old Jessica Alba to have sex with a 25 year old Jessica Alba? 60/40? 82/18? What two ages that add up to 100 would you choose?

Which celebrities do you think would be most and least appealing under the "add up to 100" rule? Sean Connery? Raquel Welch? Pamela Anderson? Michael Douglas? Helen Mirren? Orson Welles? Kirstie Alley?

Would you... have sex with any 80 year old of your choice to have sex with any 20 year old of your choice? Who would you choose for each?

WHAT'S YOUR PRICE...?

The Price of Pain

Would you... cheese-grate the skin off your knees for $15,000? $50,000? $300,000? What's your price?

Would you... iron your clothes while wearing them for $25,000?

Would you... put 1,000 staples into your body anywhere you like for $45,000? How about only 50 staples placed wherever a heartless torturer chooses?
Things to consider: Would you then remove them?

Would you... have you entire body waxed with duct tape for $2,500?

Would you... clip your tonsils with garden clippers for $750,000?

Child Rearing

The Deity is offering a special family health insurance package. In fact, you get paid for these procedures! Who says our health care system is broken?

Would you... give your 4 year old daughter Double D breast implants for $1,000,000? C-cups? B-cups? HHH cups for $50,000,000?
Things to consider: "Hey, she'll grow into them."

Would you... Botox your children every three months until the age of 21 for $300,000? For the same price, would you Botox just half of their face?

Would you... for $40,000, go to a kindergarten class and give a very clear, reasoned Power Point presentation explaining why there's no Santa Claus?

Sex Education

Would you... have sex with a manatee to have sex with all of last year's *Playboy* Playmates (men); with 10 Hollywood leading men of your choice (women)?

Would you... have sex with ten 1's to have sex with one 10? Would you have sex with five 2's to have sex with one 10? Siamese twin 5's to have sex with a 10?

How much would you... pay to have sex with Angelina Jolie (men)/Brad Pitt (women) for one night? What if he/she was suffering from herpes? A severe bout of dysentery? Tourette Syndrome?

Would you... have sex with Halle Berry (men)/Tom Brady (women) if it made you speak with a lisp for the rest of your life?

WHAT'S YOUR PRICE...?

Street Cred

Would you... street-perform in a public place for an hour if your friends promised to match the money you made times 10 (i.e. if you make $20, they give you $200)? Choose from the following talents:

Playing the spoons

Kazoo

A one person show of *Hamlet*

Grease

A hybrid of *Hamlet* and *Grease*

Erotic Dancing

Mime

Break-Dancing

Tap-dancing

You're a Poseur

Would you... pose in *Playboy/Playgirl* for $250,000? *Penthouse? Hustler? Best of Bukkake? Golden Shower Monthly?*

Which of the following would you pose in for $300,000?

Juggs?

Swank?

Plumpers?

Barely Legal?

Barely Ambulatory?

Sexual Deviant Biweekly?

Bisexual Deviant Weekly?

Bowling Wrist-Brace Fetish Monthly?

What is the most provocative publication you'd pose in for $100,000?

What's Your Poison?

Would you... drink poison ivy tea for $15,000?

Would you... use six squirts of poison ivy nasal spray for $4,000?

Would you... use two-ply poison ivy toilet paper for $7,000?

Would you... put in poison ivy-lined contact lenses for an hour for $10,000?

Would you... rinse with poison ivy mouthwash for $6,000?

Would you... wear a poison ivy yarmulke for $100?

WHAT'S YOUR PRICE...?

Lightning Round

Answer quickly without thinking.

Which of the following would you have sex with for your choice of $200,000 or the chance to have sex with any five people in the world you want:

A flounder?

A cow?

An armadillo?

A rhino?

Will Purdue?

A Winnie the Pooh hand puppet?

A baboon?

A pack of Ewoks?

$$

WHAT'S YOUR PRICE...?

9

Fast Money

Would you... sleep with your significant other's mom for $250,000 if you never got caught?

Would you... spend two months wearing a mullet for $2,000? Would there be any ramifications?

Would you... gain 150 pounds for $30,000? Like meat at the supermarket, how many dollars-per-pound would you charge and what is the max you would gain?

Would you... floss with a recently removed tape worm for $10,000?

Would you... eat a bologna-sized slice of human flesh for $1,000? $50,000? $1,000,000?

WHAT'S YOUR PRICE...?

Conscience Crushers

The Deity wants to find out who you truly are. "I'm a good person," you claim. But are you really?

Would you... write anonymous hate mail to 10 orphans saying that they will never be adopted and that no one loves them for $800,000? $500,000? $100,000? How low would you go?

Would you... run over a litter of stray kittens with a lawnmower for $75,000? $250,000? $2,000,000? What's your price?

Would you... "accidentally" bump into a four year old at a playground, knocking him over for $800?

Masturbance

Would you... masturbate with your "off" hand for the rest of life for $45,000?

Would you... masturbate with a condom on for the rest of your life for $100,000?

Would you... masturbate with "When the Saints Come Marching In" playing loudly in the background for the rest of your life of for $175,000?

Would you... masturbate to only *Good Housekeeping* magazine for the rest of your life for $300,000? *New Yorker* cartoons? Model airplane instructions? What one non-pornographic publication would you choose if you only could choose one?

$ WHAT'S YOUR PRICE...? $

Thinkers

Would you... invent a machine that accelerated all technological advances but directly caused thousands of deaths a year?
Things to consider: Would you invent the car?

Would you... invent a machine that created amazingly delicious sauces but caused 1,000 hand injures a year and killed one extremely dumb person?
Things to consider: Would you invent the blender?

Would you... invent a machine that worsened the hair of thousands of ignorant people and killed one unbelievably stupid and perverted person?
Things to consider: Would you invent the Crimper?

The Price of Humiliation

Would you... record and post audio podcasts of your sexual encounters on iTunes for $10,000? How about a recording of your bowel movements?

Would you... be publicly stripped and flogged to increase your lifespan by two years?

Would you... be publicly sodomized to increase your lifespan by ten years?

Would you... allow yourself to be publicly bar-mitzvahed to have Jay Z do a rendition of Hava Nagila at the after party?

$ WHAT'S YOUR PRICE...? $

Public Knowledge

How much would you pay to have the following things made public knowledge:

Who has fake breasts and who has real breasts

Who has had any cosmetic surgery and all the details

What happens in the afterlife

What really happened with Dave Chappelle

What really happened with O.J.

How much would you pay... for a daily tabloid (where the stories were sensationalized but true) about the people in your neighborhood?

How much if anything would you pay... to see an "outline" of your future? A four page memo hitting the highlights? A treatment? A full script?

WHAT'S YOUR PRICE...?

Bath Time

Would you... bathe daily in a tub of au jus for $500,000 (you can shower off a half hour later)? Which fluids would you bathe in daily for $500,000 deposited directly into your bank account? Answer "yes" or "no" to the following:

Nacho cheese?

Creamed Spinach?

Saliva, your own?

Saliva, a stranger's?

Saliva, Kevin McHale's?

Semen, your own?

Semen, Kevin McHale's?

Vomit?

Bile?

Liquid Feces, 50% your own, 50% Kevin McHale's?

The Name Game

Would you... change your first name to "Doodatron" for $125,000?
What about your last name?

Which of the following names would you legally change your name to for $125,000?

Scrotal McGee?

Johnny Ballcluster?

Milkbags Maximus?

Extrava Gantlabia?

The "Formerly Known as Prince" symbol?

The sound of a handful of change hitting the table?

What is the weirdest name you'd adopt for $125,000?

What's Your Price...?

In Good Company

Would you... kiss the person to your left on the lips for $20? To the right?
On the top of the breast for $40? On the side of the neck for $60?
On the taint for $500?

Would you... take a punch in the gut from the person on your left for $100?
On your right? From the first stranger you see?

Would you... kiss the next stranger you see on the lips for $100?
Decide before you see him/her.

Would you... arm wrestle everyone here, winner takes $50?

$ ($) $
WHAT'S YOUR PRICE...?

Pet Project

How much would you pay... for a pet panda cub? A pet Gizmo from *Gremlins*? A pet *Transformer*?

Would you... eat your own cat or dog for $500,000? Five million dollars? Fifty million dollars? What's your price?

Would you... die to keep your pet alive?

Would you... have sex with your dog or cat to keep it from being put to sleep? Your hamster? A three-way with your tortoise and a three-toed sloth?

The Price of Pain

Would you... let Barry Bonds take a full baseball bat swing into your gut for $10,000? $100,000? How much for a shot into your head?

Would you... jump out of a second story window for $1,000? $5,000?

Would you... jump out of a third story window for $50,000? $100,000?

Would you... hammer a nail through the back of your hand for $10,000? $50,000? $250,000?

Would you... break a finger or toe for $10,000 by snapping it? At $10,000 per digit, how many would you break?

WHAT'S YOUR PRICE...?

Mixed Blessings

Would you... want the writing prowess of Shakespeare if you could only write commercials and print ads for Reebok?

Would you... want the painting prowess of Van Gogh if you had to be a court sketch artist? A bar-mitzvah caricaturist? Would you want his abilities if you had to have his psyche as well?

Would you... want the sculpting ability of Michelangelo if you had to work in the medium of feces?

Would you... want the talent of Lebron James if you could only play against seven year old kids?

Career Change

For $300,000 a year, would you be...

A proctologist specializing in the obese and hairy?

A phone sex operator for the hard of hearing?

One of those haggard crabbing dudes on those dangerous fishing boats?

James Lipton's personal assistant?

James Lipton's personal masseuse? With "happy ending" included?

A fluffer for animal documentary films?

A toilet attendant at a constipation clinic?

Jewelry

For $5,000 a day, would you... wear a 5 lb. earring for a week? A 5 lb. nose piercing? A 5 lb. nipple piercing? A 5 lb. Prince Albert? How many days could you go for each?

Would you... wear a tongue piercing that was the size and shape of a golf ball for one week for $12,000?

Would you... wear an earring that was connected to an earring on your mother with a four foot chain for one week for $80,000? If for every foot you shorten the chain, the money is doubled how short would you go? How about your mother-in-law?

Would you... pierce your palms with pearl studs for a month for $11,000?
Things to consider: stigmata scars

WHAT'S YOUR PRICE...?

Word Problems

You have to marry someone whose weight is twice their IQ if they are a woman, and three times their IQ if they are a man. They are of average height (and not all muscle). **What IQ do you choose?**

Repeat the question above with the weight being 1.5 times the IQ for women and two times the IQ for men.

(Women) You have to have sex with a man whose penis is 1/10 (in inches) of their age. What age do you choose?

(Men) You get to have sex with someone whose bust size is half their age? What age do you choose? (Cup size is proportional and breasts are firm.)

WHAT'S YOUR PRICE...?

Barter System

Would you... trade your house with your best friend's?

Would you... trade your children with those of any other family you know? Who? What kind of asshole would do that?

Would you... trade your penis (or your significant other's penis) with someone else's? Whose?

Would you... trade your memories with a close friend's? Your sexual history? Trapezius muscles? How about your low post moves?

Bite me!

How much would it take for you to take a bite out of...

A dead rat ?

A stick of deodorant?

A live snail?

A four year old Milky Way?

Your arm?

A stranger's arm?

A corpse?

A piece of your feces?

WHAT'S YOUR PRICE...?

Mothers Day

The Deity is giving you full immunity. You'd be masked and never suspected.

Would you... body slam your mom for $30,000?

After the body slam, would you drop the elbow for another $10,000?

Then put her in a figure four leglock until she tapped out for another $8,000?

To finish her off, hit her with the Hulk Hogan leg drop for another $3,500?

Offer to help her up and then pull your hand away at the last second and give her the "psych" gesture for $12,000?

All together it comes to $63,500. How far would you go?

Final Implant

Would you... as a man, get DD breast implants for $100,000? C-cups? B-cups?

What if they can be removed after a year? After a month?

What about just one breast implant? On the top of your foot? On the bottom of your foot?

Would you... get breast implants if your significant other promised to get them too, two sizes bigger than your own? What size would you get?

WHAT'S YOUR PRICE...?

Cheers

Would you... drink a lint smoothie for $2,000?
Things to consider: the cuddly stuffed animal you'd excrete

Would you... imbibe a milkshake through an extracted fallopian tube for $1,500? $15,000?

Would you... drink a bottle of mustard for $400?

Would you... drink a glass of iced tea where the ice was frozen blood for $1,100? (Blood is disease-free). $11,000?

Anatomically Incorrect

Would you... for $1,000,000, have a finger removed? Two fingers? Two fingers and a toe? An arm? An ear? Would you have an ear added on for a million?

Would you... if the deity made it possible, have a third testicle for $100,000? If you received another $50,000 for every additional testicle you accepted, how high would you go? Things to consider: your nest egg(s); (Women: use "nipple" instead of "testicle.")

Would you... give up 1 year of your life to have a penis that was 3 inches longer (men) or breasts that were 3 sizes larger (women)? How many years for how many inches/sizes?

WHAT'S YOUR PRICE...?

Celebrity Sex
Leading Men

How much would you... pay for one steamy night with...

Tom Brady?

Justin Timberlake?

Derek Jeter?

Prince?

Vince Vaughn?

A being that is the top half of Patrick Dempsey and the bottom half of Patrick Ewing?

A trio of fast and furious Pillsbury Doughboys?

Tom Cruise?

Tom Cruise including an hour long diatribe against prescription medicine?

Celebrity Sex
Leading Ladies

How much would you... pay for one steamy night with...

Jessica Biel?

Jessica Alba?

Jessica Rabbit?

All 3 of the above Jessica's together?

Jessica Hahn?

Uncle Jesse (*Full House*)?

Uncle Jesse (*Dukes of Hazzard*)?

Okay, for the last two, how much money would you need to receive?

Would you... have sex with either Uncle Jesse to have sex with both Daisy Dukes (Jessica Simpson and Catherine Bach in her prime)?

Punch Bowl

How much would you... pay to punch (a clean shot with no repercussions)...

Paula Abdul?

Paris Hilton?

Donald Trump?

Nancy Grace?

George Bush?

Anyone who's ever appeared on the *Real World*?

On the Job

Negotiate with your friends to find a price to actually do these dares or variations thereof. (Pooling money to give is a good way to make it happen.)

Would you... for one week, change your voice mail message to you doing a freestyle rap about how you can't get to the phone for $2,000? Another $300 for beat-boxing. ***Strike a deal!***

Would you... for $3,000, plaster your cubicle or office walls with posters of *Saved by the Bell* stars? Sultry pictures of yourself? A collage of Søren Kierkegaard pictures and Mark Gastineau photos? I would. ***Strike a deal!***

Would you... for $800, stuff the crotch of you pants obscenely for the duration of the next big office meeting or presentation? (Same question for women.) ***Strike a deal!***

WHAT'S YOUR PRICE...?

Celebrity Fat Club

Would you... have sex with Angelina Jolie if she put on 50 lbs?
100 lbs?
200 lbs?
300 lbs?
How high would you go?

Would you... have sex with George Clooney if he put on 50 lbs?
100 lbs?
200 lbs?
300 lbs?
Lost 100 lbs?
Got a sex change?

The Price of Indigestion

Would you... eat a live rat for $1,000? $20,000? $100,000?

Would you... eat a Twinkie with a burrowing ant farm inside it for $6,000? $50,000?

Would you... consume a bag full of rusty thumbtacks for $100,000? $1,000,000? Things to consider: Digestion and egress

Would you... blend your left foot in a blender and consume the results for $1,000,000? $10,000,000? $100,000,000?

Would you... eat a bowl full of human placenta for $10,000? $50,000? $500,000? What's your price?

WHAT'S YOUR PRICE...?

Worst Birthday Ever

During your child's well-attended 5th birthday party, would you, for $50,000...

Do acid?

    Crack?

        PCP?

            Pot?

                Chainsmoke?

                Get very drunk?

                        Smoke opium and dress up as a
demented elderly Asian man?

Baby Names!

Don't think! Just say "yes" or "no"!
For $200,000 deposited in your bank account today, would you name your child...

Romulex?

Doctor?

Litmus?

Keldor?

Assmunch?

Whorey?

95?

Adolph?

Bigballs?

38

WHAT'S YOUR PRICE...?

Physical Pheats

If you could earn... a dollar per second by keeping your eyes closed, how long would you keep them closed for?

If you could earn... $50 every time you got slapped across the face by a stranger, what would you do to maximize your earnings?

Would you... drink a Red Bull nasally through a straw for $100? $500?

Would you... do a somersault on a bed of nails for $800? $8,000?

Would you... put ten ice cubes in your underwear until they melted for $100? Dry ice for $1,000?

Celebrity Sex Change

Would you... have sex with a creature that was half Lucy Liu/half horse? Which half would you want as the lower half and which as the upper?

Would you... have sex with a creature that had Tim Duncan's head on Pam Anderson's body? Vice-versa? Either way, how would you go about it?

Would you... have a three-way with the celebrity of your choice and the ghost of Leif Ericson?

Would you... have sex with Beyoncé if she was eight months pregnant? Albino? Lighter than air?

$ $ WHAT'S YOUR PRICE...?

Celebrity Sex Change

Would you... have sex with a five foot tall version of Johnny Depp? Four foot tall? How low would you go?

Would you... have sex with David Beckham if he sucked at soccer and was an accountant?

Would you... have sex with Bono if he wasn't in a band? What about Bryant Gumble if he had Bono's voice and talent?

Would you... have sex with a half-cyborg Denzel Washington?

The Price of Vanity

The Deity believes in humility (and humiliation). He wants to find out how vain you truly are.

Would you... never be able to look in a mirror again for $500,000? Only in fun-house mirrors? Only in car rear-views mirrors?

For the rest of your life, would you... limit your attire to various matador outfits for $350,000? $700,000? $2,000,000?

Would you... dye your hair purple for a month for $1,000? $10,000 $100,000?

Would you... have bad acne forever for $300,000? Back-ne? Crotch-ne?

WHAT'S YOUR PRICE...?

Home Sweet Home

Would you... share an apartment with Kevin Federline to lower your rent by $700 a month?

Would you... have bunk beds with Richard Simmons to live free in a three million dollar house? Would you take top or bottom bunk?

Would you... pay a $300 service fee to have your doorbell changed to Darth Vader's Imperial March?

Would you... give up TV if you could have a personal butler?

The Infamous Baldwin Page

baldwinian series/ bald WIN ee in [from Hollywood's Baldwin brothers] *n. a series of related specimens that increase incrementally in quality. The real estate agent showed the prospective buyers a **baldwinian series** of homes that culminated in a mansion.* (Definition taken from *The Yo Momma Vocabulary Builder* – **ClasslessEducation.com**)

Would you... have sex with Daniel Baldwin when he was on *Celebrity Fit Club* to have sex with Alec Baldwin in his prime? Daniel now for Billy circa *Sliver*? Stephen for Alec? Alec for Stephen? Daniel for James?

Which Alec Baldwin character would you most and least want to have sex with? Which Tom Cruise character? Will Ferrell character? Nick Cage character?

Would you... have sex with Alec Baldwin if you assumed his temper after the act?

WHAT'S YOUR PRICE...?

Give It Up!

For $100,000 deposited in your bank account today, which of the following would you give up for life?

Cereal?

Brunch?

Dishwashers?

The left sock?

All of your photos?

Memories of all the TV/movies you have ever seen?

Memories of your cousins?

The word "the"?

Running?

WHAT'S YOUR PRICE...?

The Sporting Life

Would you... pay $5,000 to be able to dunk? $25,000? How high would you go?

Would you... pay $50,000 to be able to run a sub-4 minute mile?

Would you... pay $4,000 for infallible Skee-ball accuracy?

Would you... pay $20,000 to have Larry Bird's jumpshot but Mini-Me's physical size?

Would you... pay $1,200 for ruthlessly successful Risk military strategy?

Would you... pay $1,000,000 to have Babe Ruth's baseball ability but be the spitting image of Ronald McDonald?

WHAT'S YOUR PRICE...?

Leading Ladies

How much would you pay for one steamy night with...

Jessica Simpson?

Maria Sharapova? Things to consider: grunts of passion

Natalie Portman?

Tera Patrick?

Britney Spears post-counseling? Crazy Britney?

Nicole Richie anorexic?

Nicole Richie at her normal healthy weight?

Keira Knightly?

The ghost of Rosa Parks?

WHAT'S YOUR PRICE...?
47

The Deity's Tattoo Shop

What's Your Price...?

Each tattoo has a price that represents the money you receive if you get the tattoo (and agree not to have it removed.)

Would you get a tattoo of...

The face of Roger Ebert on your right shoulder... $23,000?

All of your muscles and bones labeled as if you were a diagram in a biology textbook... $290,000?

A Hitler mustache... $700,000

The phrase "I'm with stupid" with an arrow pointing up on your chest... $115,000

A tattoo of the Deity anywhere... $4,000 (Send us a photo of your tattoo of the Deity at **info@wouldyourather.com** and we will post it on **wouldyourather.com**. and possibly publish it in the next book.)

The Chinese symbol for "cliché"... $8,000?

A full tuxedo... $400,000 (you can get this one removed)
In fact if you do, triple the money.

48

Self-Medication

Would you... attempt to remove your own appendix with a pocket knife and some rubbing alcohol for $5,000,000? With a jagged menorah and a wallet to bite down on? With your bare hands and the *Rocky* theme playing?

Would you... remove your own tonsils using any method you can, but with no help for $800,000?

Would you... attempt to self-remove a tumor in your testicle for $4,000,000 using medical textbooks, surgical tools, and a bottle of NyQuil?

Would you... surgically implant a hand grenade in your abdomen (the pin is still in it) for $75,000? $750,000? $7,500,000?

Cavity Search

For $150,000, with no chance of getting caught, but with all the physical discomfort, would you anally smuggle from an international airport, for the duration of a flight, and then through US customs...

A prune?

A plum?

A peach?

An orange?

A cantaloupe?

A celery stalk?

35 lbs. of genuine Dead Sea salt in a sealed bag that is "highly unlikely" to break?

A life size replica of the head of Louis Gossett Jr.?
Things to consider: Been there, done that.

$ $ WHAT'S YOUR PRICE...?

Breaking the Law

Would you... kill a known child molester if you could get away with it?

Would you... kill a mime if you could get away with it?
How about a mime whose whole gimmick is miming child-molesting?

Would you... commit an armed-robbery if you knew you'd never be caught?
At a bank? A 7-11? A rich asshole's house?

Would you... steal a CD if you could get away with it? Would you copy eight
mp3's from a friend? Does it make a difference how rich the musician is?

Nude to Lewd

Would you... pose naked in a magazine if someone else's face was Photoshopped onto your body for $10,000? What's your price?

Would you... pose naked in a magazine if your face was Photoshopped onto another person's more fit body for $10,000? What's your price?

Would you... be a naked body double in a hit movie for $20,000? Whose body double would you want to be?

How about a "face double" in a porno?
Go to **http://wouldyourather.com/multimedia/videos** and click on "Face Doubles" to see what this would be like.

WHAT'S YOUR PRICE...?

The Price of Never

How much would you pay... to never again get stuck in traffic?

How much would you pay... to be able to make telemarketers temporarily be unable to breathe like Darth Vadar did to his subordinates in *Star Wars*?

How much would you pay... to always smell as if you had just showered/shampooed?

How much would you pay... to have a GPS built into your brain?

How much would you pay... to have perfect mastery over English grammar?

Not Too Picky

Would you... have sex with the following for $200,000?

A sheep?

A mule?

An alligator?

A walrus?

An oompa-loompa?

A Sleestak?

Vladimir Lenin's preserved corpse?

A three-way with Lenin and a Sleestak?

A bag of croutons?

What's your price for all of the above? Go through one by one. If you answer no to all, change "have sex" to "dry hump".

54

WHAT'S YOUR PRICE...?

The Price of Discipline

Would you... limit yourself to taking 500 steps per day for a year for $10,000? How about 50 steps per day for a year for $500,000?

Would you... limit yourself to speaking 500 words per day for 1 week for $2,000? (If you go over, you lose the money.)

Would you... limit yourself to speaking 50 words per day for $10,000? If at each word under 1,000 you would receive $1,000, how many words would you speak per day?

Would you... limit yourself to consuming 500 calories per day for 1 month for $10,000?

Would you... limit your TV viewing for a year to MTV for $25,000? QVC for $100,000? Which channel would require the largest payment?

WHAT'S YOUR PRICE...?

Hair Style Chart

Would you... have the following hair or facial hair style?

	For a Week	For a Month	For a Year	Permanently
Mullet	$200	$1,000	$10,000	$100,000
Afro/Goatee Combo	$500	$5,000	$35,000	$250,000
Handlebar Mustache	$600	$7,500	$25,000	$225,000
Princess Leia Buns	$300	$5,000	$35,000	$200,000
Half Beard	$1,000	$10,000	$50,000	$400,000

What's Your Price...?

WHAT'S YOUR PRICE...?

Super Powers with a Catch

Would you... accept the power to be able to fly in exchange for weighing 500 pounds? Things to consider: landing

Would you... want X-Ray vision if you had to always wear those really, really thick "nerd" glasses?

Would you... want the power to be invisible if you always had a wet hacking cough when the power was activated?

Would you... want the ability to read minds, but only relating to deviant and perverse thoughts?

Would you... want unstoppable low-post moves if you were incapable of distinguishing between fish and self-help books?

WHAT'S YOUR PRICE...?

Family Fun

In the book *Would You Rather...?* (wouldyourather.com), The Deity posed the question, "Would you rather... watch a porno *with* your parents or *starring* your parents?" Here's a new spin on that old classic:

Would you... watch a porno movie starring your parents for $1,000? $10,000? $100,000? What's your price?

Would you... watch a porno movie with your parents for $1,000? $10,000? $100,000?

Would you... star in a porno movie and then screen it with your grandparents for $100,000? $1,000,000 for a scene with the same sex? $10,000,000 for anything involving an ostrich, a slab of beef fat, and multiple wiffle ball bats?

WHAT'S YOUR PRICE...?

Celebrity Potato Head - Women

The Deity is giving you some cosmetic surgery drawing from the body parts of celebrities. (If you are a man, consider if you would accept these exchanges for your significant other.)

Would you... want Jessica Biel's ass if you also had to have Barbara Streisand's nose?

Would you... want Salma Hayek's breasts if you also had Tina Turner's hair circa 1984?

Would you... want Elizabeth Hurley's face if you had to have Martin Scorsese's eyebrows?

Would you... want J-Lo's booty if you also had to have Jay Leno's Chin?

Would you... want Pamela Anderson's body if you also had to have her Hepatitis C?

WHAT'S YOUR PRICE...?

Give It Up!

For $10,000 deposited in your bank account today, which of the following would you give up for life?

Tomatoes?

MTV?

Gossip magazines?

Downloading music?

Watching baseball?

Smirking?

Nostalgia?

The word "very"?

Nickels?

Fashion Backward

For $100,000, would you wear, every day for a year:

A monocle?

Two monocles?

Three monocles?

A fez?

An iron fez?

An earring connected to nose piercing?

A nose piercing connected to a genital piercing? With a chain that is a little too short? Things to consider: sneezing

WHAT'S YOUR PRICE...?

All or Nothing

If you succeed, you get it all. If you fail, you get nothing!

Would you... attempt to eat 60 McDonald's hamburgers in 1 hour for $1,000?

Would you... attempt to run a marathon in under 3 hours for $500,000 (you have 1 year to train)?

Would you... attempt to hold in your bowel movements for 2 weeks for $50,000?

Would you... attempt to masturbate to orgasm 10 times in a 24 hour period for $2,400? Using only Univison programming as fodder? Using only Renaissance paintings?

WHAT'S YOUR PRICE...?

License to Drive

Would you... drive a British car for immunity to speeding tickets? The Oscar Meyer Weiner Mobile? A Trans-Am Firebird (and you always need to wear Ferrari glasses and acid-wash jeans while driving?)

Would you rather... be immune to speeding tickets *OR* parking tickets?

Would you... for $4,000,000, never be able to take a left turn ever again (with you or anyone else driving?) What about driving, walking, or any sort of left turn?

Would you... have to use hand signals for the rest of your life for $250,000?

Would you... pay a $600 service charge to make your horn that of the General Lee from the *Dukes of Hazzard*? A loud demonic voice that says "I shall destroy you?" The "Where's the Beef" line from the old Wendy's commercial?

Do Not Try This At Home

Would you... for $3,000,000, deep-fry your:

Face?

Arm?

Balls?

The southern hemisphere of your balls?

The Arctic Circle of your balls?
Things to consider: Isn't that the title of the Jonathan Krakauer book?

Would you... for $10,000, for 5 minutes, put a leech on your...

Foot?

Leg?

Forehead?

The southern hemisphere of your balls?

Personal Life

How much would you pay a week for the following:

A personal trainer?

A personal chauffeur?

A personal masseuse with a "happy ending" included?

A discrete roving personal DJ who played music to accompany your every move?

A personal swat team that watched your back, ready to spring into action at the first hint of danger?

A personal sorcerer? Who seems a little too attracted to you?

Playing the Odds
(For Men)

Would you... have sex with Jessica Biel if there was a 1 in 10 chance that her vagina would suddenly turn into a blender?

Would you... put your penis in a glory hole for $60,000 if you were told there was an equal chance of your mother, Jenna Jameson, and Greg Gumbel being on the other side?

Would you... trade your job with someone at random if there was a 10% chance they worked the late shift at a local toll-both and a 10% chance they ran a multi-billion dollar hedge fund? How about if there was a 20% chance they were a prison inmate executioner and a 20% chance they were a professional athlete?

Reading is Fund-amental

Would you... read the collected works of Shakespeare for $55,000? The entire Encyclopedia Britannica for $200,000? Every existing NBA seven-footer's autobiography for $90,000?

Would you... for $100,000, limit yourself to reading 1,000 total words per day? How about $1,000,000 for 100 words per day? How about $5,000,000 to only be able to read words that begin with the letter "q"? $10,000,000 to only be able to read this book?

The Deity has granted you a bank account with $5,000,000 in it. What's the catch? For each word you write, your bank account goes down by $100. Would you ever write again? How often?

Would you... take $1,000,000 to only be able to write words that are palindromes? How about $500,000 to have to write the word "salmon" between every three words you write?

WHAT'S YOUR PRICE...?

The Nose Knows

Would you... drink a glass of water nasally for $250? How about a shot of tequila?

Would you... smoke a cigarette nasally for $500? How about if it were an unfiltered menthol?

Would you... consume a jalapeno pepper nasally (shoving it into your nose until it falls down through your throat) for $1,000? How about a jar of extra chunky, extra spicy salsa?

Would you... have your nose surgically altered so that you have one giant nostril for $100,000? How about 5 distinct nostrils? Would you have your nose increased in size by 5000% for $5,000,000?

WHAT'S YOUR PRICE...?

Cheat Sheet

If you never got caught, would you cheat on your girlfriend or wife with...

Jenna Jameson?

Jenna Fischer?

Jenna Haze?

Halle Berry?

The Olsen Twins?

Adriana Lima?

All of the Victoria's Secret models at once?

The ghost of Harriet Tubman?

Cheat Sheet

If you never got caught, would you cheat on your boyfriend or husband with...

James Blunt?

Orlando Bloom?

Harrison Ford?

Johnny Depp?

Tony Hawk?

Steven Hawking?

All of your favorite musicians whenever you want?

Zeus?

WHAT'S YOUR PRICE...?

The Daily Grind

Would you... rollerblade to work each day for 1 year for $25,000? How about skateboard for $50,000? How about walk for $500,000? Crawl for $1,000,000?

For the "lifespan" of your current job, would you replace your morning coffee with a quadruple shot of espresso for $10,000? Three shots of Jim Beam for $100,000? How about a pint of breast milk (freshly squeezed)?

Would you... with no explanation, wear a cape to your job one day for $50? A long cigarette like *Batman*'s The Penguin? A yarmulke?

Would you... legitimately reply to every piece of spam you receive for $25,000 a year? How much would you want per piece of spam?

Personal Life

How much would you pay a week for the following:

A personal masseuse?

A personal sherpa?

A personal butler?

A personal minstrel?

A personal blues musician who appears and plays his harmonica when you start complaining?

A personal geisha?

WHAT'S YOUR PRICE...?

Dr. 9021Deity

Would you... have a sex change operation for $1,000,000? $10,000,000? $100,000,000? A race change? A species change?

Would you... get a reverse face lift (i.e. the Brent Musberger) for $85,000?

Would you... have the fat sucked from your stomach, butt, and thighs for $100,000? Oh, one more thing.... all of it is injected into your face.

Would you... have your Adam's Apple enlarged threefold for $200,000?

Would you... alter your cheeks so you always look like Dizzy Gillespie in the middle of a horn-blow for $800,000?

WHAT'S YOUR PRICE...?

Nuptials Schmuptials

The Deity moonlights as a wedding planner in order to offer an alternative to those ridiculous dominant gay guys on those wedding shows. Is he better? Well, if the price is right.

Would you... battle rap your vows for $25,000?

Would you... for $200,000, hold your wedding in a slaughterhouse? At Putt-Putt mini-golf course? At Office Depot?

Would you... for $12,000, replace the "you may kiss the bride" tradition with "you may grope the bride"?

How much would you pay... for the Pope to be your guest minister? (MC) Hammer? The team of Hammer and the Pope?

Would you... want HR Puff 'N Stuff to be your best man?

74

Indigestion Question

Would you... scarf down the contents of a bug-zapper bag for $4,500? What if you could blend it up first?

Would you... tongue clean the urinals at your favorite sports team's arena for season tickets? How about to be on the team for a game?

Would you... eat a chicken breast generously encrusted in pubic hair for $26,000? Does it in any way depend on whose pubic hair it is?

Would you... eat the "X" encyclopedia if you would remember its contents exactly? Which books/pages would you eat if eating them engrained their contents perfectly in your memory?

WHAT'S YOUR PRICE...?

The Name Game 2: Electric Booglaoo

Would you... add "De" to the front of your first name for $110,000 (i.e. Frank becomes DeFrank)?

Would you... for $120,000 change the second and third syllables of your first name to "eesha" (i.e. Amy becomes Ameesha)?

Would you... drop the first letter of your name for $22,000 (i.e. Reggie becomes Eggie)? For the same money, would you drop the last letter (Frank becomes Fran)?

Would you... change your first name to Funkalicious for $125,000?

Would you... insert a silent "b" in your name wherever you want for $6,500? Where would you insert it?

Life's a Gamble

Would you... risk your entire life savings on a coin toss if the payoff were 5 to 1? 10 to 1?

Would you... risk your left arm on a coin toss if the payoff were $5,000,000? $20,000,000?

Would you... risk your child's life on a coin toss if the payoff were $100,000,000? $500,000,000?

You make the bet! It's just one flip of the coin.

What would the payoff have to be for:

Your pet's life?

Your job?

Your marriage?

WHAT'S YOUR PRICE...?

More Punching Your Grandmother Questions

Would you... wearing a mask, punch your grandmother as hard as you can in the back of the neck once for $200,000 if she never found out it was you?

The front of the neck?

The back of the knee?

The small of the back?

Where would you punch her if you had to choose 3 spots?

Life and Death

Would you... give up 1 year of your life for $100,000? $1,000,000? How many years would you give up for what price?

Would you... give up a year of your spouse's life for $300,000? How many years would you give up for your spouse and for what price, you greedy bastard? How about your child's life? Think of the life you could give him/her for the money.

Would you... remain 17 years old for 20 years if when those 20 years were up you'd suddenly be 75? Would you remain 28 for 30 years if when those years were up you'd be 90? How old would you want to be for how long?

Would you... play jai-alai with Danny Glover for $19?

Putting the "Fun" Back in Funeral

What's Your Price...?

For $100,000 given to your family...

Would you... have an open casket funeral where people can sledgehammer you like an old car to raise additional thousands of dollars for charity?

Would you... have a Viking funeral?

Would you... be buried in your back yard (and not buried very well)?

Would you... have engraved on your gravestone, "Me Chinese, me play joke, me go pee-pee in your Coke"?

WHAT'S YOUR PRICE...?

Fantasy Peninsula

How much would you pay... to be able to get a dinner reservation anytime you wanted?

How much would you pay... to have a parking spot magically appear wherever you wanted to park?

How much would you pay... to never fart again? How about for your spouse to never fart again?

How much would you pay... to be able to bring yourself to orgasm by simply uttering the word "Romania"? How much would you pay to be able to bring anyone else to orgasm the same way?

How much would you pay... to be able to speak 10 languages fluently? How about to speak three languages—the one you currently speak, Klingon and Tolkien's Elven?

WHAT'S YOUR PRICE...?

The Price of Blasphemy

Would you... flush the pages of the Bible down the toilet for $10,000? Would you put editor's and proofreader's red ink marks all over several church copies of the Bible for $3,000?

Would you... offer a nun your rosary beads and scream "Show me your tits!" for $1,500? $15,000? $150,000?

Would you... before an Easter sermon, inflate and pass out a beach ball like they do at concerts for $500? What's your price? **Strike A Deal!**

Would you... during a sermon, cough a barely discernible "Bullshit" for $1,000? $5,000?

Would you... say "hi" to Mussolini in hell for me?

WHAT'S YOUR PRICE...?

Your Ad Here

Would you... get a four inch tattoo of a Nike Swoosh on your shoulder for $25,000? On your scalp for $250,000?

Would you... offer advertising on you gravestone if it gave those mentioned in your will $1,000 a month (increasing at the rate of inflation)?

Would you... put product placements in your every day dialogue (i.e. mention Kellogg's cereals at least 40 times a day in your every day conversations) for $100 a day? Example: "The day is as nice as Special K is crunchy! How are the kids?"

Would you... pay $150 for a page in a book like this, advertising anything you want? Email info@wouldyourather.com if interested.

Bringing Sexy Back

Would you... have sex with Leonardo DiCaprio (women)/Shakira (men) if he/she had no teeth? No teeth and no hair? No teeth, no hair, and an incurable case of the hiccups?

Would you... type left-handed for the rest of your life if you could have unlimited sex with any porn star you wanted? Would you type with your tongue for the rest of your life? With your genitals?

Would you... lose a finger to have sex with Gisele Bündchen? A thumb? A hand? An arm? A leg?

Would you... have sex with the Cocoa Puffs bird to have sex with Megan Fox from *Transformers*?

Would you... for $100,000, have sex with Janet Reno (men)/Rush Limbaugh (women) in a doggie-style position?

WHAT'S YOUR PRICE...?

Sexual Position or HathaYoga Pose?

1. Downward-Facing Dog
2. Reverse Mastery
3. Mendeleyev's Revenge
4. Asian Cowgirl
5. Deck Chair
6. Bharadvaja's Twist
7. Broken Menorah
8. One-Legged King Pigeon
9. Lord of the Fishes
10. Legs-up-the-Wall
11. Street Racer
12. Extended Triangle
13. Raised Hand to Big Toe
14. Lotus Position
15. Anal

1. Yoga 2. Sex 3. Neither 4. Sex 5. Sex 6. Yoga 7. Neither 8. Yoga
9. Yoga 10. Yoga 11. Neither (Atari game) 12. Yoga 13. Yoga 14. Sex
15. Sex

WHAT'S YOUR PRICE...?

What's Your Price...?

Day Time

How much would you pay to spend a day with...

Dick Cheney?

Tiger Woods?

George Foreman?

Stephen Hawking?

Carmen Electra?

Hillary Clinton?

George Washington?

George Washington Carver?

Gomberg?

It Pays the Bills

Would you... mop up at peep shows for $150,000 per year?

Would you... dance at an upscale strip club for $10,000 a week, tax-free? What about at a seedy strip club called Mufftown, USA where they are known to throw bottle caps and lunch meat at you?

Would you... be Naomi Campbell's personal assistant for $100,000 a year? How about Tom Sizemore's assistant? Simon Cowell's?

Would you... be a high school bus driver for $100,000 a year? A high school teacher? A pre-school teacher? A high school janitor?

Would you... be a human crash test dummy for $100,000,000 a year?

WHAT'S YOUR PRICE...?

Life's a Gamble

Are you gambler? The Deity wants to find out. Would you take part in the following coin tosses?

You Win: No more cancer
You Lose: Everyone over 40 is afflicted with cancer

You Win: You have sex with anyone you want whenever you want
You Lose: You can never have sex again

You Win: You live to 250
You Lose: You die in the next 24 hours

You Win: You can eat whatever you want without gaining weight
You Lose: Your can only consume insects

You Win: You get to be on the New York Yankees
You Lose: You get to be on the Baltimore Orioles

WHAT'S YOUR PRICE...?

The Price of Sacrifice

Would you... never go to a movie again for $1,000? $20,000? $100,000?

Would you... never eat cooked food again for $5,000? $50,000? $500,000?

Would you... never have another sexual encounter for $1,000,000?

Would you... never again use the word "fabulous" for $200?
"Baby" for $50,000? "Aardwolf" for $45? All adjectives for $900,000?

Would you... never talk again for $500,000? $5,000,000? $25,000,000?
How about if you could only talk in jive? In iambic pentameter?
Only to people over 85 years old?

The Price of Love

The irrepressible Meatloaf said, "I'd do anything for love, but I won't do that."
Evidently, no one ever named his price.

Would you... chop off your left ear if your lover said they'd leave you if you
didn't? Would you chop off your left hand?

Would you... serenade him/her with Air Supply's "All Out of Love" for $100?
How about "Baby Got Back"?

Would you... as a man, adopt your spouse's last name for $10,000?
Would you adopt your spouse's hairstyle (wear a wig if you have to) for $25,000?

Would you... wipe your spouse anytime she/he pooped for $1,000,000?

WHAT'S YOUR PRICE...?

All or Nothing

The Deity is an all or nothing sort of god. If you succeed, you get it all. If you fail, you get nothing!

Would you... attempt to drink 1 gallon of water in 2 minutes for $500?
1 gallon of orange juice for $1,000?

Would you... attempt to eat a can of SPAM in 1 minute for $6,000?

Would you... attempt to live on the streets of NYC for 1 year for $1,000,000?
Would you watch that if it was a reality TV show?

Would you... attempt to get a book published for $2,500? If you have a good concept, email it to info@falls-media.com.

WHAT'S YOUR PRICE...?

Religious Experience

Would you... be willing to live homeless and with no material possessions or offspring if it meant you could live for 500 years?

Would you... want to receive an expiration date on your birth certificate to know your death date?

Would you... convert to any other religion for $100,000? $1,000,000?

Would you... devoutly and publicly worship McDonald's Hamburglar for $5,000,000? How about if you had a vision that he was the one true God?

WHAT'S YOUR PRICE...?

Dining for Dollars

Which of the following would you eat for $1,000?

A live worm?

A calf eyeball?

This book?

A pubic hair sandwich?

A bowl of lice?

Which of the following would you eat for $10,000?

A rusty razor blade?

A partially developed duck embryo?

A horse rectum?

A live gecko?

10,000 calories a day for one month (you choose the food)?

Public Restroom Etiquette

How much would you pay your friend to complete these dares:

Go over to a guy using a urinal and share it?

Stand about 6 inches farther away from a urinal than is standard?

Stand about 36 inches too far (explain you're working on your range)?

Take a dump in a urinal like Randy Quaid did in the movie *Kingpin*?

For more ideas like this, check out our book *Do Unto Others* (astonishingly close to being out of print, but not quite).

$ WHAT'S YOUR PRICE...?

And You Thought Algebra Was Useless

You are going to have a threesome. Mazel Tov. The conditions are that your partners need to total a height of 14 feet. How do you divide the height of your partners? How do you go about your activity?

You are going to have another threesome. Mazel Tov, once again. This time the weight of your partners must equal 500 pounds. How do you divide the weight? How do you go about your activity?

You are going to have a sexual free-for-all with 10 members of the opposite sex at once. Big-time Mazel Tov. This time the total height can equal 20 feet. How do you divide the height? How do you go about your activity?

Maximum Security

Would you... spend a day/night in a maximum security prison for $10,000 (your cellmate is in for armed robbery)?

Would you... spend a day/night in a maximum security prison for $100,000 (your cellmate is in for sexual assault)?

Would you... spend a day/night in a maximum security prison for $5,000 (your cellmate is in for impersonating Geoffrey Chaucer)?

Would you... voluntarily lock yourself up in a maximum security prison for 10 years if at the end of those 10 years you received $10,000,000? What about minimum security?

Would you... share a cell for a year with Meadowlark Lemmon for $100,000?

WHAT'S YOUR PRICE...?

Manly Sports

Would you... play a game in the NFL with your current talent and build without a helmet for $35,000? Without a cup for $10,000? If you got an additional $10,000 for every yard gained?

Would you... return a punt while blindfolded in an NFL game for $15,000?

Would you... go 1 round with Mike Tyson, in order to go 1 night with Carmen Electra? 2 rounds for 2 nights? How many rounds if there is no knock-out or TKO?

Would you... get into the ring with Muhammad Ali (past) for 60 seconds for $50,000? Muhammad Ali (present day) for $500?

Would you... let Roger Clemens throw a fast ball at you for $5,000? (You're allowed to avoid the ball, if you can.)

WHAT'S YOUR PRICE...?

Commissioned Works

How much would you pay to have...

Matt Groenig base a *Simpsons* character on you?

a character based on you in the game *Warcraft*?

Bob Woodward write your biography? Stephen King? The head writer for *Penthouse Forums*?

Tarantino direct your life-story? Your daydreams?

Heimberg and Gomberg write a *Would You Rather...?* question about you?

WHAT'S YOUR PRICE...?

Evil Inclinations

Would you... commit these crimes for money if you would never be caught:

Would you... egg your parent's house for $25,000? At $500 per egg, how many eggs would you throw at their house?

Would you... drown a cat for $100,000? At $100,000 per cat, how many would you drown?

Would you... burn down an old age home for $500,000 (assume the home is empty)?

Would you... email death threats to your spouse for $20,000? How about leave death threats to your spouse via voicemail for $100,000?

WHAT'S YOUR PRICE...?

DeitTV

The Deity is in charge of his own network and has some interesting programming in mind.

Would you... want to have a reality show based on your workplace? Your neighborhood? Your life back in high school?

Would you... pay $10,000 to see your life story on the big screen with all of the people from your life played by your favorite stars? Who would you get to play whom? What would be the soundtrack?

Would you... accept the challenge to debate your choice of Hillary Clinton, George Bush or Flavor Flav on national TV?

Would you... take $100,000 for all of your erotic dreams to play on public access TV at 3am each night?

WHAT'S YOUR PRICE...?

The Price of Sleep

Would you... limit your sleep to 4 hours per day for the rest of your life to earn $250,000 per year for doing so? 3hours? 2 hours? 30 minutes?

Would you... sleep each night hanging up side down like a bat, for $500,000? For the same price, would you sleep standing up leaning against a wall? Only while in transit?

Would you... have all your dreams be silent movies for $100,000?

Would you... sleep a night in a room with an eerie but harmless live clown lurking in the corner for $1,000?

Balls (as in courage)

Would you... headbutt an unleashed Doberman Pincher for $1,000? $10,000?

Would you... be stuck in a six by six room with a venomous snake for 1 hour for 100,000? With a clarinet? With a stick? With a pair of furry dice and some Vaseline?

Would you... fill a dozen Ziploc bags with oregano and try to smuggle them onto a plane for $5,000? How about a dozen Ziplocs filled with sugar for $10,000?

Would you... take a shower in a maximum security prison for $5,000?

Would you... run into a burning building to try save a cat for $20,000? A child for $100,000? A safe that has a 50% chance of containing $1,000,000 for $250,000?

Would you... step in and try to negotiate peace between rival groups of Bloods and Crips as they approach each other for a rumble for $250,000?

WHAT'S YOUR PRICE...?

102

What's In a Name?

Would you... have sex with every celebrity named "Janet" to have sex with every celebrity named "Eva"?

Would you... have sex with every celebrity named "Dennis" to have sex with every celebrity named "George"?

Would you... want to have sex with every celebrity named "Tori"?

Would you rather... have sex with every celebrity named "Kate/Katie" *OR* "Jennifer"? "Jessica" *OR* "Cindy"? "Hillary" *OR* "Oprah"?

Would you rather... have sex with every celebrity named "Ted" *OR* "Al"? "Bruce" *OR* "Vince"? "Jamie" *OR* "Regis"?

Playing the Odds

Would you... eat a random piece of a cake that had a dead mouse somewhere inside it for $1,000? $10,000?

Would you... drink a margarita off a table that has 10 margaritas on it, if one of the margaritas had cyanide instead of salt on the outside of the glass for $5,000,000?

Would you... run across an open field holding a metal rod during a lightning storm for $25,000? $100,000?

Would you... try to land a 747 for $10,000,000? With others on board?

WHAT'S YOUR PRICE...?

Ouch

Would you... take a swift strike from a ball-peen hammer on the penis head for $400?

Would you... hole-punch your tongue for $8,000?

Would you... have your scrotum cut open and filled with wasps for $600,000?

Would you... take a drug that causes the hair on your head to grow inward for $1,000,000? The hair on your face? The hair on your body?

Leading Men

How much would you pay for one steamy night with...

Jared Leto?

James Franco?

David Beckham?

Tom Brady?

Pelé?

Brad Pitt?

Tom Hanks?

Jon Bon Jovi?

Jay-Z?

Daniel Craig?

WHAT'S YOUR PRICE...?

Sex, Drugs, and Defenestration

Would you... have sex with every "after" photo of someone in a weight loss commercial if you had to have sex with the "before" as well?

Would you... become a crack addict for 1 year if you were given $5,000,000 one month into your addiction? What if you were given the money after your year and a stint in rehab?

Would you... be defenestrated from a second story window for $8,000?

Would you... be fenestrated into a first story window for $50?

Perversion Excursion

Would you... have sex with Scarlet Johansson (men) /Josh Duhamel (women) if your foreplay had to include a Dirty Sanchez?

Would you... have sex with Heidi Klum (men)/ Heath Ledger (women) if the sex had to include an Arabian Goggles?

Would you... have sex with your favorite model/actor if they were wearing a Nixon mask?

Would you... get a "jelly doughnut" from Don Rickles for $380,000?

Minor League Baseball Team or Deviant Sex Act?

Columbus Clipper?
Toledo Mud Hen?
Cleveland Steamer?
Topeka Destroyer?
New Orleans Zephyr?
Tucson Sidewinder?

Answers: Cleveland Steamer and Topeka Destroyer are sex acts; the rest are baseball teams.

WHAT'S YOUR PRICE...?

What's Your Price....?

Specifically Speaking

When depositing your bi-weekly payroll check, would you have it immediately doubled if you agreed to take a tremendous diarrhea in your pants while in the bank lobby? While wearing just Umbro shorts?

For a free lifetime membership to the most expensive country club in your neighborhood, would you spend your first day at the pool wearing a bathing suit made of Saran Wrap?

For men, would you accept a 30% increase in pay (but no guarantee on your employment) if, during all business meetings and social functions, you were required to wear those white comfy nurse shoes?

Making Your Parents Proud

Would you slyly masturbate to the point of orgasm...

On a plane for $2,000?

At a Starbucks for $3,000?

In the audience at a Broadway show for $2,500? While performing in a Broadway show for $50,000?

During a funeral for $5,000?

While driving for $2,000?

While getting a haircut for $25,000?

Stunt Double

Would you... jump out of a car moving at 10 miles per hour for $500? 30 mph for $10,000? At $100 per mph, what's the fastest you'd go and jump?

Would you... hole punch your earlobe for $5,000? How about the skin between your thumb and index finger for $25,000? Your glans/labia for $500,000?

Would you... dip your finger for 2 seconds into a pot of boiling water for $500? Would you stick your whole hand into a pot of boiling water and hold it there for 20 seconds for $10,000? Would you swallow a glass of boiling water for $25,000?

Would you... attempt to swim across the English Channel for $250,000?

Would you... fight a retarded cougar to the death if the winner gets $1,000,000?

WHAT'S YOUR PRICE...?

Abstention

Would you... abstain from the following?
Use the chart as a starting point to strike a deal.

	For a Week	For a Month	For a Year	Permanently
Bathing	$200	$4,500	$45,000	$1,000,000
Brushing your teeth	$50	$3,000	$15,000	$1,000,000
Carbohydrates	$500	$7,500	$60,000	$2,000,000
Watching TV	$500	$5,000	$25,000	$500,000
Sexual contact	$250	$5,000	$50,000	$2,500,000
Drinking	$100	$500	$10,000	$100,000
Email	$500	$5,000	$50,000	$2,000,000

WHAT'S YOUR PRICE...?

Fun with Adhesives

Would you... Krazy Glue your pinky and ring finger together for two days for $250? Your thumb, index finger, ring finger and pinky all to your palm for $1,000? Simulate that now.

Would you... Krazy Glue your palms together for a day for $2,000? Your shoes onto your feet for $5,000? Pubic hair clippings onto your lips for $7,000?

Would you... papier-mâché your entire body for $500? $3,000?

Would you... believe that "papier-mâché" is automatically spell-checked and accented properly when you type it in Microsoft Word? Good work, Gates.

WHAT'S YOUR PRICE...?

The Price of Ink

It's time to get another tattoo. Once again, the price is what you receive for getting inked.

Your choice of a major U.S. city's subway map... $10,000?

A pocket protector and pens over your left breast... $16,000?

The face of William Shatner on your crotch... $50,000?

The crotch of William Shatner on your face... $100,000?

The Chinese symbol for "Chinese symbol"... $1,000?

The Chinese symbol for "I'm just trying to get laid"... $11,000?

What is the weirdest tattoo you'd get? What word would you get if you had to get one word? What quote? Maybe "There are no time-outs in the world of professional wrestling." Just an idea.

That's Pranksta

The Deity, as you might have realized, likes to mess with people's minds. Will you help him on his quest?

Would you... initiate an all-out food fight in a five star restaurant for $1,000?

Would you... dress up and pretend to be a trainer at a health club for $100?

Would you... substitute iced tea into a 40 ounce bottle of Old English and sip it as you work for $200?

Would you... "draw a charge" in a mall from a random passer-by for $30? At $10 per additional charge, how many would you take? **Strike a deal!**

Would you... draw a charge from someone in Foot Locker and then complain to an employee for $100?

WHAT'S YOUR PRICE...?

Stopwatch

Would you... watch your grandparents have sex for $10,000? $100,000? What's your price?

Would you... watch the long-lost Roseanne Barr Tom Arnold sex tape for $3,000?

Would you... watch Rosie O'Donnell go to the bathroom for $300? Diarrhea for $2,000? Would you watch Rosie O'Donnel do anything at anytime for any amount of money?

Would you... watch a stranger be eaten by a lion for $25,000? $100,000? What's your price?

Pain, Pain, Go Away

What's Your Price...?

Would you... smoke a poison oak cigarette for $20,000?

Would you... eat a four inch by four inch piece of honeycomb covered in bees for $4,000?

For $250,000, would you... swallow and pass a Rubik's cube? An extra $500,000 if you can solve it while passing it?

Would you... let a dentist give you a root canal with no anesthesia for $10,000? $50,000?

Would you... let a proctologist give you a colonoscopy with no sedative or medication for $20,000? Would you let a dentist give you a colonoscopy and a proctologist give you a root canal for $100,000?

$ 👤 $

WHAT'S YOUR PRICE...?

Potluck

Would you... give away your life's savings to have a 100 mile per hour fastball?

Would you... walk with a limp for rest for life for $500,000? Walk with a pimp strut? A speed-walk? A moonwalk?

Would you... pay $10,000 to add 1" to your penis? $50,000? $500,000? How much would you pay per inch? How many inches would you add? Women: read this as "Would you pay $ for your spouse/boyfriend/lover to add..."

Would you... grow an afro with a four inch radius for $1,000? 8 inch radius for $10,000? 16 inch for $100,000?

Would you... allow each of your sexual partners to rate your performance in bed on the Internet for $10,000?

Celebrity Potato Head - Men

The Deity is giving the men some cosmetic surgery drawing from the body parts of celebrities. (If you are a woman, consider if you would accept these exchanges for your significant other.)

Would you... want LL Cool J's physique if you had to have Judd Nelson's nostrils (still your nose)?

Would you... want John Holmes' penis if you also had to have Hulk Hogan's current hair?

Would you... want Matthew McConaughey's abs if you also had to have Donald Trump's hair?

Would you... want Brad Pitt's face if you also had Yao Ming's arms (the rest of your body is it's current size)?

Would you... want Gene Simmon's tongue?

120

Going Abroad

Don't think, say yes or no!
For $1,000,000, would you accept permanent banishment to the following places, never being able to leave:

Tonga?

Canada?

South Central Los Angeles?

Narnia?

Antarctica?

The Mall of America?

Heimberg's living room?

What's your price for each of the above?

WHAT'S YOUR PRICE...?
121

Care to Go for a Swim?

Would you... go for a fifteen minute swim in a pool of phlegm for $1,000? $10,000? $100,000?

Would you... spend 10 minutes in a pool filled with Great White Sharks for $100,000?

How about if you had an open slow bleeding cut out of your Achilles tendon?

How about if the Great Whites had all had their teeth removed prior to your time spent in the pool?

Would you... spend 10 minutes in a pool filled with Waterbugs for $500? Rats for $25,000? Rabid Trix Rabbit clones for $50,000?

WHAT'S YOUR PRICE...?

All or Nothing

The Deity hangs out with Michael Vick and not surprisingly likes to put on fights for show. And so these are the circumstances: Winner takes home $1,000,000, and the fight is to the Death.

Would you fight...

Two Gary Colemans?

A blind gorilla?

Ryan Seacrest?

100 bullfrogs?

A ninja who is also looking for his keys at the time?

1,000 Weebles?

Three sentient beach umbrellas?

WHAT'S YOUR PRICE...?

Odd-Fashioned

For 370,000 tax free dollars, would you... for the rest of your life, wear a piano tie to all formal occasions including business meetings, weddings, and funerals?

Would you... wear a T-shirt that said "Certified Muff Diver" to the office on Casual Friday for $22,000? What about semi-transparent white slacks under which you have briefs emblazoned with "The Fartbeat of America"?

What is the most ridiculous thing you'd wear to the office for a day for $5,000?

For $25,000, while attending a family reunion, would you... wear cut-off Daisy Duke jean shorts with an inch diameter crotch seam? What are the shortest cut-off jeans you'd wear for $25,000 as measured by crotch diameter?

WHAT'S YOUR PRICE...?

Dare Devil

Would you... go to the gym and complete your workout with a helmet, knee pads and elbow pads for $100? $500? $1,000?

Would you... ask a barber to shave your chest for $200 (you only get the money if they do it)?

Would you... use the term "ape-shit" ten times in one day at work or on a first date if your friends gave you $100? At $5 per additional "ape-shit", how many would you say? ("Ape-shit's" must be confirmed).

Would you... object to the marriage at a wedding for $1,000? $10,000? (You just need to state your objection once; you don't need to stop the marriage).

Would you... object to a funeral for $20,000?

WHAT'S YOUR PRICE...?

Well, Pierce My Brosnan

Would you... pierce your nipples for $1,000? $10,000? What's your price? Name everywhere you'd pierce for $1,000? What's your pierce?

Would you... get a taint piercing the size of a pearl for $100,000? The size of a marble? The size of a super ball? A piercing of a key ring with your keys permanently on it?

Would you... for $2,500, pierce your ear with a toothpick (you have to get all the way through)? A Capri Sun straw? A screw?

Would you... get a piercing anywhere with a working grandfather clock pendulum for $100,000? Things to consider: Why don't they have earrings with moving parts like turning gears or something? Transformer earrings? Puzzles? It's a completely untapped market.

Would you... wear cat embryo earrings for a day for $1,000? $10,000? What's your price?

WHAT'S YOUR PRICE...?

Fun in the Sun

Would you... go to the beach in a string thong and Tevas for the whole afternoon for $900?

Would you... bury your body in the sand with just your head protruding for 3 hours for $3,000? Same thing with just your balls protruding (you have a breathing tube)?

Would you rather... spend a 90 degree day at the beach in a string thong *OR* a wool sweater and ski pants?
(Check out questions like this at **wouldyourather.com**.)

Would you... tan half of your body by wearing a special suit for a week at the beach for $500? What strange tan-line would you do for $500? Farmer's tan? Inverse Farmer's tan?

Putting Yet More "Fun" in "Funeral"

What's your price to wear the following to a funeral of a close family friend:

An oversized retro football jersey?

Leather pants?

One of those "#1" foam hands?

An incredibly tight miniskirt, feather boa, and heavy make-up?

A military uniform even though you weren't in the military?

All denim?

Colonial garb?

Any of the Village People's outfits? Which one would you choose?

The Sporting Life

Would you... take a charge from Shaq for $500?

Would you... take a free kick to the nuts by David Beckham for $1,000?

Would you... get drilled with a blind-sided tackle by Joey Porter for $2,000?

Would you... get hit in your unprotected chest with a Mario Lemieux slapshot for $5,000 and a new found ability to spell all French words and names?

Would you... take a croquet shot in the foot by Ernie "The Hammer" Kerchanski for $25?!

The Price of Envy

How much would pay to be the following for one day and why...

Guys

Bono?

Tom Brady?

Steve Carell?

David Beckham?

Hugh Heffner?

Tim Russert?

George Washington?

Gary Gnu?

Women

Paris Hilton?

Perez Hilton?

Laura Bush?

Kelly Clarkson?

Queen Elizabeth?

Angelina Jolie?

Cleopatra?

Mrs. Bono?

WHAT'S YOUR PRICE...?

Indecent Proposals

The Deity liked that movie *Indecent Proposal*. It inspired him to pose the following questions.

Would you... if your spouse agreed, and there were no repercussions thereafter, let a disease-free stranger have sex with your spouse once for $1,000,000?

Would you... let this same debonair stranger dry-hump your spouse awkwardly for 4 minutes in a back seat of a Chevy for $60,000? "2 minutes in the closet" for $20,000?

Would you... if she agreed, accept $1,000,000 for the same stranger to deflower your 18 year old daughter?

What if that stranger was Dikembe Mutombo?

Fitness Challenge

The Deity moonlights as a personal trainer. He likes any job where he can demean and belittle mortals, and here's his motivational technique. Regarding the tasks below, if you can do it, you get a $100, if not, you pay $100.

Would you... try to do 100 push-ups in 5 minutes?

Would you... try to do five pull-ups in a row? Ten?

Would you... try to run a mile in under 7 minutes?

Would you... pay $1,000 to get to your target weight with a snap of your finger? $10,000? $100,000? How much if the weight change was permanent?

Note: This page has been certified as filler by the Federal Literary Authority (FLA).

WHAT'S YOUR PRICE...?

Ye Olde Masturbation Page

Would you... for $400,000, give up masturbating for the rest of your life?

Would you... for $300,000, have to masturbate the rest of your life with closed fists?

Would you... for $600,000, only be able to masturbate in JC Penny stores? Radio Shacks? People named Mervin's homes?

Would you... for $700,000, masturbate the rest of your life with your feet?

Would you... never make another easy masturbation joke again for $100,000?

Gross Price

Would you... for $2,000, fully use bath and face towels that had never been washed in the ten years a hotel's been open?

Would you... be thrown up on (your neck and chest while wearing a tank top) for $300?

Would you... drop an earthworm in your ear for $1,000?

Would you... consume a vomit Popsicle for $5,000? How about a Crapsicle for $50,000?

Would you... tongue clean the armpits of all the Seattle Supersonics players after each basketball game for 1 season for $500,000?

Would you... lick the top of an ant hill for $250? $2,500?

Moral Dilemmas

You are assured by the Deity that if you push one of your parents in front of an oncoming train, world hunger would end. Do you do it?

You are offered a chance to prevent anyone else in the world from smoking. The catch: you have to smoke 3 packs a day. Do you take up the habit?

While having a cocktail at a bar, you notice a friend's husband sitting with a woman, holding hands and having a drink. Do you mention it to your friend?

You've already sold your home. As you are leaving, you realize that the toilet floods whenever flushed. Do you have it fixed?

Immoral Dilemmas

You snap up two excellent seats on a bus and save one, hoping the attractive person you see in line will ask for it. An old lady asks first. Do you punch her in the face or the stomach?

An unbelievably attractive spouse of a close friend offers you the chance for a one-time "no one will know" affair. Do you partake in oral or anal sex?

Your cat has been lost for three months. You discover that neighboring small children found your beloved pet injured in a ditch, paid $150 for veterinary care and adopted it. When you take your cat back, do you call the kids "lonely dorks" or "petless losers?"

California grape pickers are on strike and organizing a boycott for unfair labor conditions. The store only has California grapes and you want some. When you make your wife go out and get the grapes, do you tell her to also pick up a *Hustler* magazine or chewing tobacco?

WHAT'S YOUR PRICE...?

Meaningless

Would you... sit on a bowl of green beans for an hour for $120?

Would you... pay $60 to play one round of Boggle with Gary Sinise?

Would you... belly-flop off the low diving board to understand how to correctly use the word "vouchsafe"?

Would you... take the name of your spouse upon marriage if it were "Destructo"?

Would you... like to find your true passion in life if it were throwing ladles into a river?

Deity Boutique

Which of the following would you wear for 1 week straight for $1,000? $10,000?

A Superman costume?

Swim goggles?

Nothing but a black leather g-string?

A sombrero?

A pirate's eye patch?

A suit made from cow fat?

A Storm Trooper costume?

Your spouse's wardrobe?

Brass knuckles?

138

Potpourri

How much would you pay... to have feet that adjusted to fit comfortably to any shoe that you put on?

How much would you pay... to be able to make all racists suddenly turn into minorities?

How much would you pay... to be able to orally gratify yourself?

How much would you pay... to never forget anything you ever read?

How much would you pay... to be capable of changing your eye color at will?

How much would you pay... for that muffler? A lot?

WHAT'S YOUR PRICE...?

You're Covered

Would you... have all your toes surgically removed for $200,000? Your nipples for $100,000? How about your arms for $1,000,000? What body parts for what price?

Would you... have your eyelashes permanently removed for $5,000?

Would you... have miniature ivory elephant tusks implanted in your face for $20,000,000?

Would you... have a shark's fin added to your back for $1,000,000?

Would you... give your left nut for all the tea in China?

140

I Never

For $1,000,000, which of these would you never do again?

Shave?

Eat chocolate?

Look at any form of porn?

Listen to music?

Kill an insect?

Control your bladder?

Wash your hands? Face? Genitals?

Talk to an immediate relative (of your choosing)? Who would it be?

Sleep between the hours of 3 and 4 AM?

Worship Ralph Sampson?

WHAT'S YOUR PRICE...?

Conscience Crushers

Would you... let the panda bear go extinct if you were given $300,000?

Would you... curse out your parents for no reason for $100? $1,000? Your grandparents?

Would you... give a 12 year old stranger a line of cocaine for $100,000?

Would you... step in front of an 8 year old to catch a foul ball at a baseball game if you knew you'd catch it?

Would you... intentionally drive over the foot of a pedestrian for $10,000?

Would you... slip some milk into a severely lactose intolerant friend's coffee for $500?

Would you... grab a Sikh's turban and sprint away, giggling like a schoolgirl, for $250?

WHAT'S YOUR PRICE...?

Your Better Half

How well do you know your significant other?

Would he/she... blog your sex life for $1,000 a week? $10,000?

Would he/she... have a threesome with Angelina Jolie?

Would he/she... ever get any type of plastic surgery? What if it was free? And painless?

Would he/she... steal from any type of store if there was no chance he/she would be caught?

Would he/she... pose naked on an Internet site for $100,000?

WHAT'S YOUR PRICE...?

The Price of Fame

What's Your Price...?

How much would you pay... to have a cameo appearance on *Grey's Anatomy*? Is there any show you'd pay to have a small speaking part on?

How much would you pay... to be a finalist on *American Idol*? How about to be a judge for one show? How about to be a fly on the wall at Paula Abdul's home?

Would you... want to be as famous as Lindsey Lohan if you were as troubled by drugs and alcohol as she is?

How much would you pay... to be the new voice of Mr. Moviefone? Your choice of the new face of Aunt Jemima syrups or Uncle Ben's rice? A new monster in Dungeon and Dragon's *Monster Manual*?

$ WHAT'S YOUR PRICE...? $

Office Space

Would you... for $250,000, have to forever and with no exceptions use the business email farty-farts@gmail.com?

Would you... tell your boss exactly what you thought of him/her (holding nothing back) for $10,000? $100,000?

For a 250% increase in salary, but no job security, would you insist on having all business meetings in your office in a retro two-seater arcade driving game?

Would you... when a group of important clients come in, greet everyone you meet by kissing their hands for $500? Sniffing their butts like dogs for $5,000? Grabbing their genitals, giggling and bouncing up and down for $25,000?

WHAT'S YOUR PRICE...?
145

Playing the Percentages

How much would you pay... to be 5% faster?

10% taller?

25% thinner?

50% younger?

75% funnier?

100% smarter?

1,000% stronger?

WHAT'S YOUR PRICE...?

A-hole

Would you... trip a waiter as he or she walked by with a tray full of food for $300? Would you laugh hysterically for an extra $100?

Would you... for $1,000, go to a junior high school, wait outside, and then when a nerdy kid walks out, walk past him and knock his books down in front of everybody, then walk away, never to be seen again?

Would you... sit in the bleachers and heckle the outfielders at a Special Olympics softball game for an inning for $3,000? $30,000? $300,000?

Would you... surreptitiously set the home page of all your co-workers' computers to messyhandjobs.com for $250? $2,500?

WHAT'S YOUR PRICE...?

Question Excerpted from Shakespeare

What's Your Price...?

Would you... submerge your hand for 30 seconds in a just-used public toilet (that was just flushed) for $100? Unflushed for $1,000?

How much would you pay... to never have diarrhea again?

Things to consider: Do you ever kind of like it?

How many days would you not wipe your ass, at $500 per day?

How many days would you forego deodorant, at $500 per day?

How many days would you forego washing and cutting your hair at $500 per day?

WHAT'S YOUR PRICE...?

148

Sex with Celebrities
by Milton Bradley

Would you... have sex with Siamese twin versions of Taye Diggs (women)/
Eva Longoria (men)?

Would you... pay $300 to take a charge from Jessica Simpson?

Would you... pay $1,000 to receive oral sex from Scarlett Johansson?
How about if she had a cold sore on her lip? How about a cold sore, strep
throat, and a Hitler moustache?

Would you... accept or pay money to mutually masturbate with Aretha Franklin?

Would you... shave your head to have brunch with Jennifer Love Hewitt?
Dinner with Vince Vaughn? Name your celebrity, name your meal.
Name what you'd shave.

$ $
WHAT'S YOUR PRICE...?
149

Absurditron 8000

Would you... loiter at a Michaels Craft store twice daily if it would contribute to the reincarnation of J.R.R. Tolkien?

Would you... keep your pants constantly stuffed with kelp if it increased your vertical leap by ten inches?

Would you... shed your skin once a year for a complete understanding of the mechanism that causes grass stains?

Would you... get a bowl cut in exchange for the ability to do origami with your mind?

Projected audience for this page: 12

Age Limits

Would you...

want to live to 1,000 and have your IQ be 30?

want to live to 30 and have your IQ be 1,000?

want to live to 300 and always be 400 pounds?

want to have the strength of a 25 year old when you're 90 if you'd have the neck of a 90 year old when you're 25?
Things to consider: ascots

(D&D nerds only) want to have a 17 Wisdom but only an 8 Charisma?

WHAT'S YOUR PRICE...?
151

Leftovers

Would you... stay in bed for a year for $100,000?

Would you... nestle your face in a sumo wrestler's post match butt-crack for $10,000?

Would you... sacrifice 2 "points" of your child's looks for $100,000 (so if your child was an 8 out of 10, they'd be reduced to a 6)? $1,000,000? How about at $100,000 per point, how many points?

Would you... sacrifice 20 points of your child's intelligence for $100,000? $1,000,000? How about at $100,000 per point, how many points?

Would you... allow yourself to be hit by a car going 10 mph for $25,000? Would you allow yourself to be hit by a car going 25 mph for $500,000? What speed for what price?

$ ( ) $
WHAT'S YOUR PRICE...?

Getting Personal

Would you... give a full body massage and oiling to (insert unhygienic friend) for $250?

Would you... share a weekend in Amish country with (someone you hate) for $500?

Would you... manually gratify (insert friend's relative) for $100,000?

Would you... be limited to reading (insert book title) the rest of your life for $100,000?

Would you... wrestle (insert someone else in the room with you) if the loser had to be the other's slave for a day? **Strike a deal!**

WHAT'S YOUR PRICE...?

Getting Really Personal

Would you... put (insert elderly relative or acquaintance) in a full nelson at full pressure for a minute for $5,000? Half nelson?

Would you... have sex with (insert someone you know who is gross) four times in a night for $10,000?

Would you... let (someone in room) cut your hair however they want for $100? $500? Strike a deal.

Would you... email nude photos of yourself to (insert co-worker) for $25,000?

Would you... confess feelings of love to (NBA seven footer) in a YouTube video?

WHAT'S YOUR PRICE...?

You've Got the Power

How much would you pay... to never again have your cell phone reception go out?

How much would you pay... to be able to, at your will, give people hiccups? Orgasms? Afros?

How much would you pay... to always know for sure when someone is lying to you?

How much would you pay... to have the ability to see through tinted windows? Polyester? Linoleum? Fudge?

How much would you pay... to have the power to know what someone looks like just by hearing their voice?

WHAT'S YOUR PRICE...?

A Close Shave

Would you... shave your head for $100? $1,000? $10,000?

Would you... shave with a shard of glass and some lathered soap for $500? $5,000?

Would you... shave your eyebrows for $1,000? $5,000? What's your price?

Would you... shave all of your body hair (completely) for $1,000? $5,000? What's your price?

Would you... shave your spouse's head in their sleep for $10,000? (You'd never be caught.)

Would you... let someone pull out all your pubic hair by hand for $15,000? Would you burn it off with lighter fluid, matches and a candle snuffer for $80,000?

WHAT'S YOUR PRICE...?

Disorderly Conduct

The Deity is quite the therapist. You come in for a visit, you leave with money (and a new psychological issue).

Would you... for $400,000, suffer from a type of Tourette Syndrome that causes you to randomly exclaim statistics of former NBA seven footers?

Would you... take $1,500 to have a mental block that prevents you from ever understanding the concept of a "baker's dozen"?

Wludo ouy... eb ldixscde orf ?oo5oo$

Would you... for $200,000, suffer from Post-Traumatic Stress Syndrome? What about Pre-Traumatic stress syndrome, where you're so neurotic, you become crippled with fear of the various traumas that could occur?

$ 🧔 $
WHAT'S YOUR PRICE...?
157

Dead White Guys

The Deity is resurrecting a famous genius of history for just along enough to give you a special gift.

How much would you pay... to have Van Gogh paint your portrait? Picasso? Bob Ross (the "Happy Trees" guy)?

How much would you pay... to have Ernest Hemmingway write a short story based on an incident of your life? Which incident would you choose?

How much would you pay... to have Michelangelo sculpt your image?

How much would you pay... to have Noam Chomsky write leftest propaganda about you?

WHAT'S YOUR PRICE...?

Gratuitous Surgery

Which of the following surgeries would you have if you didn't need them for $200,000?

Rotator cuff surgery?

An appendectomy?

Hip Replacement surgery?

Gastric Bypass surgery?

Hymen Restoration surgery (women) / Foreskin Restoration surgery (men)?

Hair graft onto your head? Your back? Your calves?

Let Loose

Would you... flash your breasts at the band during a heavy metal concert for $250? At the orchestra during a philharmonic concert for $2,500? At a church during a sermon for $10,000?

Would you... at a book signing, ask a revered conservative author of historical biography to sign your breast for $200? $1,000?

Would you... attempt to suck on the toes of a stranger at the beach for $500?

Would you... stare intensely at the cleavage of any woman you interact with over the course of a day for $500? $5,000?

Would you... tip a stripper with change, if your fat frat buddy promised to give you five times the amount you were able to get the strippers to accept over the course of a night?

$ $
WHAT'S YOUR PRICE...?

Random Associations

Would you... leave your year old child for the day with Ozzy Osbourne for $1,000? Simon Cowell? Andy Dick?

Would you... cut your salary by 5% to have a Casual Friday? Thong Thursday? Girls Gone Wild Wednesday? Tonka Truck Tuesday?

Would you... let Barney butt-ball you if it increased the chance of your eternal salvation by 15%? Is there any "puppet" you'd let do it to you just for the hell of it?

Would you... restrict yourself to bartering for goods for the duration of a relationship with Salma Hayek?

WHAT'S YOUR PRICE...?
161

Would You Rather...?

The Deity is up to his old tricks. He offers you $100,000, and this time, he gives you the choice of two options for it.

Would you rather... be roommates for a year at college with Judas Priest (the rock group) *OR* Judas Priest (the Biblical guy)?

Would you rather... for the rest of your life, have to wear the clothes that you wore at age 17 *OR* that you will wear at age 70?

Would you rather... sneeze inward *OR* fart inward?

Would you rather... always move around in a fast and jerky fashion as if in an old home movie *OR* only be sexually aroused by umpire balls and strikes calls?
www.wouldyourather.com

162

Doo-doo, Pee-pee, and Existential Quandaries

Would you... drink a mugful of water from a toilet with urine in it for $500?

How much money would it take to photograph your poop and use the picture as your Christmas card? (You must send it to everyone you know.)

Would you... to paraphrase Jean-Paul Sartre, exert your autonomous will only if you first accept that you must count on no on but yourself; that you are alone, abandoned on earth in the midst of infinite responsibilities, without help, with no other aim than the one you set yourself, with no other destiny than the one you forge for yourself on this earth?

Fine Dining

Would you... eat a pair of cooked elephant testicles for $5,000?
Raw elephant testicles for $10,000?

How many live cockroaches would you eat in one sitting for $1,000 per roach?

Would you... eat a stick of butter in one minute for $200?

Would you... drink a pig fat milkshake for $250?

Would you... eat a bowl of earwax sherbet for $5,000?

WHAT'S YOUR PRICE...?

Phone Matters

Would you... call up (insert set of friend's parents), state your name, and have two minutes of anonymous phone sex for $1,000? $10,000? What's your price?

Would you... drunk dial your boss for $1,000? $3,000? $7,000? Would you drunk dial your boss every night for a week for a new Mercedes?

Would you... always answer the phone with a riddle and only have a conversation if the caller answers correctly for $200,000?

Would you... use a 1985 cell phone for a year (reception is fine) for $20,000?

WHAT'S YOUR PRICE...?

About The Authors

Would you... for an unreliable income that could potentially develop into something substantial, write below your intelligence in a way that entertains some people and alienates others including your relatives, and meets little of your creative ambition and desire to affect the world in a meaningful way?
Things to consider: Would you be Justin Heimberg?

Would you... want to be a horrible aberration seemingly drawn from a lunatic's nightmares, resembling a writhing mass of grey flesh covered with dozens of randomly placed eyes and mouths, of different sizes and shapes; not being regarded as an evil creature as such, but in order to sustain your mad self, forced to feast upon the bodily fluids and sanity of mortal creatures, preferably intelligent ones, attacking by spitting strings of protoplasmic flesh which end in a mouth and one or more eyes at opponents, which then bite them, causing both acid and blinding damage?
Things to consider: Would you be David Gomberg?

www.falls-media.com • www.wouldyourather.com

About the Deity

The ringmaster/MC/overlord of the *Would You Rather...* empire is "the Deity." Psychologically and physically a cross between Charles Manson and Gabe Kaplan, the Deity is the one responsible for creating and presenting the WYR dilemmas. It is the Deity who asks **"Would you rather... watch a porno movie with your parents or a porno movie starring your parents?"** And it is the Deity who orders, without exception, that you must choose. No one knows exactly why he does this; suffice to say, it's for reasons beyond your understanding. The Deity communicates with you not through speech, nor telepathy, but rather through several sharp blows to the stomach that vary in power and location. Nearly omnipotent, often ruthless, and obsessed with former NBA seven-footers, the Deity is a random idea generator with a peculiar predilection for intervening in your life in the strangest ways.

About the Font

This font Scala Sans is an asshole, virtually impossible to work with. Total diva, always wanting to be made bold and enlarged. What a prick, seriously! Kept talking shit about Times New Roman and Courier as sell-outs, and spreading false rumors that Century Gothic was gay. We would constantly hear shouting from its trailer, only to find demure female fonts like Brush Script running out alarmed, exclaiming "That is disgusting!" So Scala Sans font, up yours! You suck!

Other *Would You Rather...?*® Books:

Would You Rather...?: Love & Sex asks you to ponder such questions as:

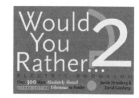

- **Would you rather...** orgasm once every ten years OR once every ten seconds?

- **Would you rather...** have to have sex in the same position every night OR have to have sex in a different position every night (you can never repeat)?

- **Would you rather...** have breast implants made of Nerf® OR Play-Doh®?

- **Would you rather...** have sex with the new Daisy Duke (Jessica Simpson) OR classic Daisy Duke (Catherine Bach)?

- **Would you rather...** vicariously experience all orgasms that occur in your zip code OR during sex, have the Microsoft paper clip help icon appear with sex tips?

Would You Rather...?: Love & Sex can be read alone or played together as a game. Laugh-out-loud funny, uniquely imaginative, and deceptively thought-provoking, *Would You Rather...?: Love & Sex* is simultaneously the authors' most mature and immature work yet!

Would You Rather...?® 2: Electric Boogaloo
Another collection of over three hundred absurd alternatives and demented dilemmas. Filled with wacky wit, irreverent humor and twisted pop-culture references.

Available at www.wouldyourather.com

More Books by Falls Media

The Official Movie Plot Generator

"A Coffee Table Masterpiece" - *Newsweek*.

The Official Movie Plot Generator is a unique and interactive humor book that offers 27,000 hilarious movie plot possibilities you create, spanning every genre of cinema from feel-good family fun to hard-boiled crime drama to soft core pornography. Just flip the book's ninety tabs until you find a plot combination you like. For movie fans or anyone who likes to laugh a lot with little effort, *The Official Movie Plot Generator* is a perfect gift and an irresistible, offbeat diversion.

Pornification

"For every legit movie, there exists (at least theoretically), a porn version of that movie." *Pornification* includes over 500 "pornified" titles, along with hysterical quizzes, games and challenges. There's something for everyone, from *Cold Mountin'* to *The Fast and Bicurious* to *Malcolm XXX*, so open up and enjoy!

Available at www.wouldyourather.com

Would You Rather...?: Illustrated — Tired of having to visualize these dilemmas yourself? No need anymore with this book of masterfully illustrated ***Would You Rather...?*** dilemmas. Now you can see what it looks like to be attacked by hundreds of Pilsbury Doughboys, get hole-punched to death, sweat cheese, or have pubic hair that grows an inch every second. A feast for the eyes and imagination, ***Would You Rather...?: Illustrated*** gives Salvador Dali a run for his money.

Would You Rather...?: Pop Culture Edition
A brand new collection of deranged dilemmas and preposterous predicaments, featuring celebrities and trends from popular culture. Ponder and debate questions like: *Would you rather... be machine-gunned to death with Lite-Brite pegs or be assassinated by Cabbage Patch Dolls?*

Would You Rather...?'s What Would You Be?
Stretch your metaphor muscles along with your imagination as you answer and discuss thought/humor-provoking questions like: If you were a Smurf, which one would you be? What if you were a type of dog? A road sign? A Beatle? A nonsense sound?

Got Your Own *Would You Rather...?* Question?

Go to **www.wouldyourather.com** to submit your question and share it with others. Read and debate thousands of other dilemmas submitted by the authors and users.

www.wouldyourather.com

Featuring:
New *Would you rather...?* questions:

More humor books and games

More *Would You Rather...?* products

Comedy videos, writing, animations and more!

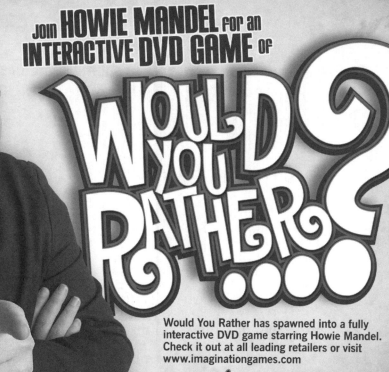
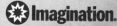